WORKBOOK

FOR

(A GUIDE TO CHRIS VAN TULLEKEN'S BOOK)

Ultra-Processed

People

A Guide to Why We Can't Stop Eating
Food That Isn't Food

Strategist Monroe

WORKBOOK FOR Ultra-Processed People

Table of Contents

Introduction:

CHRIS VAN TULLEKEN'S describes their experience in a laboratory where they participated in a journal club. During these sessions, lab members would present scientific papers and engage in critical discussions about the research. The author highlights the importance of scientific argumentation and the training they received in the lab.

The lab's focus was on the competition between viruses like HIV and the cells they infect. This competition resembles an arms race, with cells developing defenses against viral attack and viruses evolving better weapons to overcome those defenses. The author mentions a splinter group within the lab that studied a different type of virus found in human DNA, often referred to as "junk" DNA. A paper presented in journal club revealed that these seemingly inactive viral genes are actually engaged in an evolutionary arms race with other genes in the genome.

The implications of this arms race within our genes are significant. It suggests that the human genome is constantly evolving to keep these viral genes suppressed, leading to greater complexity. The author suggests that this internal arms race may be the driving force behind the evolution of complexity itself.

The author then transitions to their current research focus on the food industry and its impact on human health. They argue that the act of eating is also an arms race for energy, with various life forms competing for limited resources. However, the introduction of ultra-processed foods (UPF) in the modern diet has disrupted this natural competition. UPF, which makes up a significant portion of the average diet in many societies, has been linked to detrimental effects on human health, the environment, and society.

The author emphasizes the need to understand and address the harms caused by UPF consumption, including obesity. They acknowledge the complexity of the issue and the tendency to blame individuals for their weight. The author challenges this blame by highlighting the influence of genetics and the impact of the food environment on weight gain.

Overall, this passage sets the stage for the author's exploration of the detrimental effects of ultra-processed foods and the need to re-evaluate our food culture.

Part One: WAIT, I'M EATING WHAT

1.

Why is there bacterial slime in my ice cream? The Invention of UPE

The author, accompanied by an industry insider named Paul Hart, explores the reasons why UPF, such as ice cream, contains ingredients like stabilizers, emulsifiers, gums, and various oils. These ingredients help in the mass production, distribution, and preservation of UPF while keeping the costs low.

The use of stabilizers, emulsifiers, gums, and oils in ice cream serves several purposes. Firstly, they make the ice cream more tolerant of temperature changes during transportation and storage. This allows for easier handling and distribution throughout the supply chain. Additionally, these ingredients help prevent the formation of ice crystals and maintain a creamy texture by holding water close to them. By doing so, ice cream can be produced in large quantities in centralized factories and then transported to various locations, reducing costs and logistical challenges.

The author also discusses the economic factors that contribute to the prevalence of UPF in the diets of countries like the UK and the USA. Factors such as low wages, time constraints, and the promise of convenience and taste contribute to the consumption of UPF, which is often cheaper and easier to obtain than foods prepared at home. The author mentions that the high levels of economic inequality in these countries may be linked to the higher consumption of UPF compared to other high-income nations.

Moreover, the author and Paul Hart delve into the molecular composition of UPF and how it differs from traditional, minimally processed foods. UPF often replaces real and expensive ingredients with cheaper alternatives and additives. For example, synthetic carbohydrates derived from crops grown for animal feed are used as replacements for starches found in traditional foods. These modified alternatives can mimic the properties and functionalities of original ingredients, allowing for cost reduction and widespread use in UPF production.

In summary, this passage highlights the reasons behind the presence of bacterial slime in ice cream and the use of various additives in UPF. It also touches upon the economic factors and molecular composition that contribute to the widespread consumption of UPF in certain countries.

Workbook:
Engaging Discussion Questions:

1. Have you ever noticed unusual ingredients in processed foods? How does the presence of additives impact your perception of the food's quality?

----

2. What do you think are the main reasons behind the widespread use of ultra-processed

foods in our diets? How does economic inequality contribute to this trend?

----

3. How do you think the food industry balances cost-saving measures with maintaining the taste and texture of processed foods?

----

4. Do you believe that the emphasis on convenience and low cost in our food choices outweighs the potential negative health effects of ultra-processed foods? Why or why not?

Lessons:

➢ The presence of additives, stabilizers, emulsifiers, and gums in processed foods is indicative of ultra-processed foods (UPF). These ingredients contribute to the extended shelf life, ease of production, and cost-saving measures implemented by the food industry.

➢ Economic factors, such as low wages, time constraints, and the promise of delicious taste, contribute to the high consumption of UPF in countries with economic inequality.

➢ UPF often replaces expensive ingredients with cheaper alternatives, which are often synthetic or extracted from crops grown for animal feed. This molecular replacement is the foundation of ultra-processed food production.

➢ Understanding the chemistry of synthetic carbohydrates, such as modified starches, helps to comprehend the diverse properties and applications of these ingredients in UPF.

Guides:

➤ Guide to Identifying Ultra-Processed Foods: Learn how to read ingredient labels and identify the presence of additives, stabilizers, emulsifiers, and gums, which are common indicators of ultra-processed foods.
➤ Guide to Making Healthier Food Choices: Explore strategies for making informed decisions when it comes to selecting and purchasing food products, with an emphasis on reducing consumption of ultra-processed options.

Action Steps:

➤ Conduct a pantry audit: Examine the food items in your pantry and identify any ultra-processed foods. Consider replacing them with healthier alternatives or exploring homemade options.
➤ Experiment with homemade recipes: Choose a favorite ultra-processed food

item and find a recipe to make it from scratch using whole ingredients. Document the process and compare the taste and nutritional value to the store-bought version.

Journal Prompts:

➢ Reflect on your personal consumption of ultra-processed foods. How often do you rely on them in your daily diet? Are there specific factors that drive your food choices?

➢ Describe a memorable experience where you discovered unusual or concerning ingredients in a processed food product. How did this experience impact your perception of processed foods?

➢ Imagine a future where ultra-processed foods are less prevalent. How do you envision the food industry adapting to meet consumer demands for healthier options?

➢ Explore your relationship with convenience foods. What role do they play in your busy lifestyle? Are there ways to incorporate healthier alternatives without sacrificing convenience?

2.

I'd Rather Have Five Bowls of Coco Pops: The Discovery of UPF

In this chapter, the author describes his initial encounter with ultra-processed foods (UPF) through his daughter's desire for Coco Pops, a highly processed cereal. Despite his reservations, the author allows his daughter to have the cereal and observes her consuming it in a trance-like manner, unable to control her eating. Intrigued by this experience, the author begins researching UPF and comes across two important papers. The first paper introduces the NOVA system, a classification of food based on the extent and purpose of processing, which categorizes UPF as a separate group. The second paper presents an experiment showing that an ultra-processed diet leads to increased calorie intake and weight gain compared to an unprocessed diet. Intrigued by these findings, the author decides to conduct a month-long UPF diet experiment with the help of a colleague. The chapter concludes with the author's preparations for the experiment, including eliminating UPF from his diet and undergoing baseline measurements and tests.

Discussion Questions:

1. How did the author's observation of his daughter's eating behavior with Coco Pops contribute to his interest in studying UPF?

----

2. What are some examples of processed culinary ingredients mentioned in the NOVA classification system? How do these ingredients contribute to the overall nutritional value of food?

----

3. How does the author's encounter with the NOVA system challenge the prevailing understanding of food and nutrition?

----

4. Why do you think UPF is not mentioned in national nutrition guidelines or labeled as such on food packaging in the UK and the US?

----

5. What were the key findings of Kevin Hall's experiment on ultra-processed diets, and how

did they support the theory proposed by Carlos Monteiro?

----

6. How does the author's decision to conduct a month-long UPF diet experiment demonstrate the scientific method and the importance of pilot studies?

Lessons:

> Our perceptions of food and nutrition can be influenced by packaging,

marketing, and societal norms, which may not always align with the actual healthfulness of a product.

➤ Processing plays a significant role in the composition and effects of food, and understanding the extent and purpose of processing can provide insights into its impact on our health.

➤ Scientific research and collaboration can help uncover hidden relationships between diet, processing, and health outcomes, challenging prevailing beliefs and paving the way for further investigation.

Guides and Action Steps:

➤ Familiarize yourself with the NOVA system and its classification of food groups to develop a better understanding of processed and ultra-processed foods.

➤ Take a critical look at food packaging and labels, considering the nutritional information and marketing claims to make informed choices about the foods you consume.

➤ Experiment with preparing meals using unprocessed or minimally processed ingredients to incorporate more nutritious options into your diet.

> ➢ Support research and initiatives aimed at raising awareness about the impact of ultra-processed foods on health and advocating for clearer food labeling and guidelines.
> ➢ Share your knowledge about UPF and the potential risks associated with their consumption with friends, family, and community members to promote informed decision-making about food choices.

Journal Prompt:

Reflect on your own eating habits and the role of ultra-processed foods in your diet. Consider the following questions and write down your thoughts:

> ➢ How often do you consume ultra-processed foods? Can you identify any specific products or meals that fall into this category?
> ➢ What factors influence your decision to choose ultra-processed foods? Is it convenience, taste, advertising, or something else?
> ➢ How do you feel after consuming ultra-processed foods? Do you notice any differences in your energy levels, mood, or overall well-being?

➢ Have you ever tried to reduce your intake of ultra-processed foods? If so, what strategies did you use, and how successful were you?

➢ Are there any concerns or doubts you have about the impact of ultra-processed foods on your health? What information or research would you like to learn more about?

➢ Reflect on the role of marketing and packaging in influencing your food choices. How do colorful labels, appealing characters, and nutritional claims affect your perception of a product's healthiness?

Take your time to answer these questions honestly and thoughtfully. Use this opportunity for self-reflection and to gain a deeper understanding of your relationship with ultra-processed foods.

3

Sure "Ultra-Processed Food" Sounds Bad, But is it Really a Problem?

In this chapter, the author, Chris Van Tulle ken, discusses his personal experience on a camping trip with his brother and brothers-in-law while following an ultra-processed food (UPF) diet. He reflects on the negative effects of UPF on his well-being and imagines the impact of UPF on his blood. Later, the author receives a call from BBC Radio to make a documentary about UPF, which leads him to contact Kevin Hall, a prominent figure in nutrition science. Hall initially dismisses the concept of UPF but decides to conduct an experiment to disprove it. The experiment involves comparing two diets: one consisting of 80% UPF and the other with 80% unprocessed foods. Surprisingly, the participants on the UPF diet consumed 500 more calories per day and gained weight, while those on the unprocessed diet actually lost weight. Hall's experiment provides strong evidence supporting the hypothesis that UPF contributes to weight gain and obesity. The findings have significant implications for nutrition research and have sparked further scientific interest in the relationship between UPF and health.

Workbook:

Discussion Questions:

1. Have you ever experienced negative effects, such as weight gain or decreased well-being, as a result of consuming ultra-processed foods? Share your experiences with the group.

----

2. Do you believe that the marketing and packaging of ultra-processed foods play a significant role in their consumption? How can these marketing strategies be addressed to promote healthier eating habits?

----

3. How does the cost and time involved in preparing unprocessed meals impact people's food choices? What can be done to make healthier options more accessible and convenient?

----

4. How does the experiment conducted by Kevin Hall challenge the traditional

WORKBOOK FOR Ultra-Processed People

understanding of nutrition science? What implications do these findings have for public health policies and dietary guidelines?

Lessons:

➢ Ultra-processed foods can have negative effects on health, contributing to weight gain and obesity.
➢ The marketing and packaging of ultra-processed foods can influence consumer choices and lead to overconsumption.
➢ Unprocessed foods, prepared with whole ingredients, can support weight loss and improved well-being.

➢ The cost and time associated with preparing unprocessed meals can be barriers to healthier eating habits.

Action Steps:

➢ Assess your own diet and identify any ultra-processed foods you consume regularly. Consider healthier alternatives and try to reduce your intake of UPF.

➢ Pay attention to marketing tactics used by food companies and critically evaluate their claims. Choose whole, unprocessed foods and avoid falling for misleading advertisements.

➢ Experiment with preparing meals using whole ingredients and explore new recipes that prioritize fresh fruits, vegetables, lean proteins, and whole grains.

➢ Advocate for policies and initiatives that promote access to affordable, unprocessed foods in your community. Support local farmers' markets and initiatives that provide fresh, nutritious options to underserved areas.

Journal Prompts:

➢ Reflect on a time when you made a conscious effort to eliminate or reduce ultra-processed foods from your diet. How did this change affect your physical and mental well-being?

➢ Describe a favorite unprocessed meal or snack that you enjoy. What makes it satisfying and nourishing for your body?

➢ Consider the influence of marketing and packaging on your own food choices. Have you ever been swayed by clever advertising? How can you become more discerning as a consumer?

➢ Write about a personal goal related to improving your diet and reducing the consumption of ultra-processed foods. What steps will you take to achieve this goal, and how will you measure your progress?

4.

(I Can 't Believe it' s Not) Coal Butter: The Ultimate UPF

The chapter begins by recounting the controversial history of Imhausen-Chemie, a German chemical company involved in various illicit activities, including producing ecstasy and assisting in the construction of a poison-gas factory in Libya. The company's president, Jürgen Hippenstiel-Imhausen, known as Hippi, was a defiant figure who denied any wrongdoing. However, the darker history of the company traces back to its origins in 1912 when it started manufacturing chemicals, including explosives, during World War I.

The narrative then shifts to the development of synthetic food, specifically coal butter, during World War II. German scientists Franz Fisher and Hans Tropsch devised a method to convert low-quality coal into liquid fuel, which left behind a by-product called paraffin. Arthur Imhausen, the founder of Imhausen-Chemie, saw an opportunity to turn paraffin waste into edible fat due to Germany's shortage of fats and oils. With the help of Wilhelm Kepler, a politician connected to the Nazi regime,

Imhausen established the Deutsche Fettsäure Werke to produce synthetic fat. Through further chemical processes and the addition of diacetyl, water, salt, and beta-carotene, they transformed the fat into a butter-like substance known as coal butter.

The chapter highlights the ethical issues surrounding synthetic foods, as they require extensive testing to ensure safety, often using human and animal subjects. In the case of coal butter, tests were conducted on over 6,000 prisoners in concentration camps. Despite potential health risks, the synthetic fat was approved for consumption, particularly by U-boat crews during the war.

The narrative then explores the nature of corporations, focusing on the legacy of Imhausen-Chemie and its connections to IG Farben, a notorious German company involved in war crimes during World War II. Despite the atrocities committed, the company continued to operate after the war, and its subsidiaries eventually transformed into well-known companies such as BASF, Bayer, and Hoechst.

The chapter concludes by examining corporations as organisms within an ecosystem driven by money. It suggests that mere shame and outrage are inadequate for limiting the survival and behavior of complicit companies. The analogy between corporate survival and biological arms races highlights the need to divert the flow of money to effect change.

Discussion Questions:

1. How do you think the history and controversies surrounding Imhausen-Chemie reflect the ethical challenges faced by corporations in the pursuit of profits?

----

2. What are some potential long-term health and environmental impacts associated with the production and consumption of synthetic foods?

----

3. Do you believe that the flow of money is the primary driver of corporate behavior? How can individuals and society influence this flow to promote ethical practices?

Lessons:

➢ The production and consumption of ultra-processed foods can have ethical, health, and environmental implications.
➢ Corporations may prioritize profit over ethical considerations, necessitating increased scrutiny and regulation.

➤ Synthetic foods often lack the cultural and historical meaning associated with traditional foods, reducing food to a technical substance.
➤ Recognizing the power dynamics within the corporate ecosystem can help shape strategies for promoting ethical practices.

Action Steps:

➤ Educate yourself about the ingredients and processing methods used in the production of ultra-processed foods.
➤ Choose whole and minimally processed foods whenever possible, prioritizing natural and nutritious options.
➤ Support local and sustainable food systems to promote cultural and historical food practices.
➤ Advocate for transparent labeling and stricter regulations on the production and marketing of ultra-processed foods.

Journal Prompts:

➤ How has reading about the history and controversies surrounding Imhausen-Chemie affected your perspective on the food industry and ultra-processed foods?

➢ Reflect on a time when you consumed an ultra-processed food product. How did it make you feel physically and emotionally? Did this chapter influence your thoughts or feelings about that experience?

➢ Consider the cultural and historical significance of food in your own life. How does the industrialization and mass production of food affect this significance? Are there any traditional or cultural food practices that you would like to preserve or explore further?

➢ Imagine a future where synthetic foods dominate the market. How do you think this would impact our health, environment, and society as a whole? What steps can individuals and communities take to prevent or mitigate this scenario?

Remember, small steps can lead to significant change. By educating ourselves, making conscious choices, and advocating for a more ethical and sustainable food system, we can contribute to a healthier and more meaningful relationship with the food we consume.

PART TWO: But can't I just control what I eat?

5.

The Three Ages of Eating

In the chapter the author explores the historical context of eating. He divides eating into three distinct ages that overlap with each other. The first age involves living organisms consuming non-living substances like rocks and metals, a process that has been occurring since the beginning of time. The second age involves organisms eating other living organisms, possibly after some processing. This has been happening for millions of years, with humans engaging in this type of eating for around 2 million years. The third age, which is relatively new, involves a single species (humans) and their pets and livestock consuming ultra-processed foods (UPF) created using industrial techniques and novel molecules.

The chapter delves into the early history of the Earth, explaining how the conditions may have been milder than previously thought, with evidence of liquid water present around 4.4 billion years ago. It discusses the emergence of life around 3.5 billion years ago, evidenced by microfossils and bacterial deposits. The chapter also explores the fundamental processes of how life captures energy by passing electrons from food to breath.

The author emphasizes the interconnectedness of organisms and ecosystems, highlighting the role of the first recorded trace of eating's second age found in fossils known as Dickins onia rugs. These fossils demonstrate that eating is not just about acquiring energy but also about preparing other life to be eaten and actively changing the ecosystem.

The chapter further discusses the complexity of eating, as organisms need to fulfill two needs simultaneously: providing energy and providing construction materials for the body. It explains the precise requirements of various elements and minerals for complex organisms like humans and animals, and the challenge of obtaining these through diet. The author explores how herbivores, such as cows, have evolved mechanisms to balance energy intake with toxin load and acquire a diverse diet by learning and memorizing interactions with different plants.

Workbook:

Discussion Questions:

1. How has the third age of eating, characterized by the consumption of ultra-processed foods, impacted society's health and well-being?

----

2. How do the three ages of eating demonstrate the interconnectedness of organisms and ecosystems?

----

3. In what ways do you see the principles of the second age of eating, involving the consumption of other living organisms, reflected in modern food systems and dietary choices?

----

4. How can an understanding of the three ages of eating help us make more informed choices about our diets and food consumption

----

Lessons:

➢ The history of eating spans three ages, each with its own characteristics and impacts on human health and the environment.

➢ Eating is not just about acquiring energy; it is a complex process that involves preparing other life to be eaten and actively changing ecosystems.

➢ Understanding the precise requirements of various elements and minerals in our diets can help us make informed choices about what we eat.

➢ Herbivores have evolved mechanisms to balance energy intake, toxin load, and nutrient requirements through a diverse diet and learning from their experiences.

Action Steps:

➢ Evaluate your own eating habits and consider the extent to which your diet includes ultra-processed foods.

➢ Explore ways to incorporate more diverse and nutrient-rich foods into your meals.

➢ Educate yourself about the nutritional requirements of your body and how different foods contribute to meeting those needs.

WORKBOOK FOR Ultra-Processed People

6.

How Our Bodies Really Manage Calories.

In this chapter, the author explores how our bodies regulate food intake and manage calories. They discuss the internal system that has evolved over millions of years to regulate energy intake and body fat. Humans naturally have a higher body fat percentage compared to other land mammals. Obesity is rare in populations that still live in the "second age of eating" where food is obtained through hunting and gathering. However, the rapid increase in obesity since the 1900s, especially among children, is a significant concern.

The author explains that the idea of weight regulation is relatively new, and many assumed that humans had lower body fat percentages in the past due to limited food availability. However, the regulation of weight is similar to other physiological parameters in the body, such as water balance and breathing, which are precisely controlled internally. The author discusses experiments conducted on rats, where damage to the hypothalamus, a part of the brain responsible for maintaining homeostasis, led to uncontrolled eating and obesity.

The regulation of food intake involves complex systems that operate below our conscious level. Hormones like leptin play a role in long-term weight control and communicate with the brain to signal hunger or fullness. Additionally, various organs, including the liver, pancreas, and intestines, interact with the brain to regulate food intake and energy balance.

The author also delves into the connection between the pleasure of eating and the body's regulation of food and energy. The two systems, one guiding eating for pleasure and the other overseeing eating for nutrition, are intricately linked. The author highlights that the current food environment, filled with ultra-processed foods (UPFs), disrupts our ability to self-regulate and may affect our evolved mechanisms for weight regulation.

The chapter concludes by discussing the energy balance model, which attempts to unify the various factors influencing weight regulation. It emphasizes that eating is not simply a conscious choice and that external cues and signals, both inside and outside the body, greatly influence food intake and energy balance. The author notes that simplistic advice to "eat less and move more" is ineffective for sustained weight loss and highlights the complexity of the issue.

Discussion Questions:

1. How does the regulation of food intake differ between humans and other animals?

----

2. What are some of the external factors that influence our food choices and eating behaviors?

----

3. Do you believe that the current food environment disrupts our ability to self-regulate? Why or why not?

----

4. How can an understanding of the body's weight regulation systems help in addressing the issue of obesity?

Lessons:

➢ Our bodies have evolved to regulate food intake and energy balance, similar to other physiological parameters.

➢ Hormones like leptin play a role in long-term weight control and communicate with the brain to signal hunger or fullness.

➢ Eating is influenced by complex systems operating below our conscious level, involving both biological and environmental factors.

➢ The current food environment, particularly ultra-processed foods, may disrupt our evolved mechanisms for weight regulation.

Action Steps:

➢ Pay attention to your body's hunger and fullness cues. Listen to your body and try to eat in response to physical hunger rather than external cues.

➢ Make conscious choices about the types of foods you consume. Opt for whole, unprocessed foods whenever possible.

➢ Limit exposure to external cues that may influence your eating behaviors, such as food advertisements or tempting food displays.

➢ Stay informed about the impact of ultra-processed foods on health and consider reducing their consumption in your diet.

7.

Why it isn't About Sugar.

In this chapter the author discusses the role of sugar and carbohydrates in weight gain. The chapter begins by introducing Gary Taubes, a well-known figure in the nutrition field who proposed that carbohydrates, not dietary fat, are responsible for weight gain. Taubes argued that the hormone insulin plays a crucial role in hunger and fat storage. According to his theory, consuming carbohydrates causes a spike in insulin levels, leading to increased fat storage and decreased energy expenditure. Taubes believed that reducing carbohydrate intake would result in weight loss and improved metabolic health.

The chapter then explores the evidence supporting and contradicting Taubes' hypothesis. While Taubes' ideas gained popularity and influenced dietary trends such as the ketogenic diet, scientific studies have provided mixed results. One study conducted by Kevin Hall, as part of the Nutrition Science Initiative (NuSI), aimed to test Taubes' hypothesis. However, the results did not support the notion that calories from sugar promote more weight gain than calories from fat. Hall concluded that a calorie is a calorie, regardless of the source.

The chapter also discusses other studies that have examined the effects of low-carb and high-carb diets on weight loss and metabolic health. Some studies found no significant difference in calorie intake between low-carb and high-carb diets, while others reported greater weight loss on high-carb diets. Furthermore, real-world experiences suggest that low-carb diets are challenging to sustain in the long term.

The chapter concludes by acknowledging that while Taubes' hypothesis attracted attention, it has not been consistently supported by scientific evidence. The author notes the importance of conducting rigorous studies with pre-specified analysis plans to reduce bias. The personal experience of the author and studies on ketogenic diets for epilepsy also indicate that low-carb diets may not be sustainable for everyone.

Workbook:

Discussion Questions:

1. Have you ever followed a low-carb or ketogenic diet? What was your experience like, and did you achieve your desired results?

----

2. How do you think societal beliefs about sugar and carbohydrates influence our dietary choices?

----

3. Do you agree with the notion that a calorie is a calorie, regardless of its source? Why or why not?

----

4. What factors do you think are most important in maintaining a healthy and sustainable diet?

Lessons:

- ➤ Scientific hypotheses should be tested through rigorous studies with pre-specified analysis plans to reduce bias.
- ➤ Personal experiences and anecdotal evidence may not always align with scientific findings.
- ➤ Dietary strategies should be sustainable in the long term to achieve lasting health benefits.
- ➤ Multiple factors, including lifestyle, genetics, and individual preferences, contribute to weight gain and weight loss.

Action Steps:

- ➤ Evaluate your own dietary habits and consider whether reducing carbohydrate intake aligns with your personal goals and preferences.
- ➤ Consult with a healthcare professional or registered dietitian to develop a balanced and sustainable eating plan.
- ➤ Stay informed about the latest research on nutrition and critically evaluate popular dietary trends.
- ➤ Focus on overall dietary patterns rather than demonizing specific nutrients, such as sugar or carbohydrates.

Journal Prompts:

> ➢ Describe your experiences with different diets or dietary patterns. How did they affect your weight, energy levels, and overall well-being?
> ➢ Reflect on the role of carbohydrates in your current diet. Do you believe they contribute to weight gain or other health issues? Why or why not?
> ➢ Consider the influence of societal messages and media on your dietary choices. How do you navigate conflicting information about nutrition?
> ➢ Explore your personal beliefs and attitudes toward weight, body image, and health. How do these beliefs

8.

...Or About Exercise

In this chapter from the book the author discusses the common perception that obesity is primarily caused by a lack of exercise. He presents arguments from various studies and experts that challenge this belief. The author mentions the work of Steven Blair, Peter Katzmarzyk, and James Hill, who argue that inactivity plays a more significant role in weight gain than the consumption of ultra-processed foods (UPF). These researchers propose that increasing physical activity can offset excess calorie intake and reduce the need for food restriction.

The author refers to a study by James Hill, suggesting that increasing physical activity can counteract the effects of a poor diet. Another study by Peter Katzmarzyk demonstrates that a lack of physical activity is a major predictor of childhood obesity. The author acknowledges the importance of the relationship between calorie intake and expenditure, highlighting that consuming more calories than burned leads to weight gain. However, he questions the assumption that reduced physical activity is the primary cause of weight gain, especially considering the decrease in overall calorie consumption in the UK.

The author examines a paper by Christopher Snowdon, which argues that the rise in obesity is primarily caused by a decline in physical activity rather than an increase in sugar, fat, or calorie consumption. Snowdon's paper uses UK government data to show a decline in calorie and sugar consumption alongside an increase in obesity rates. However, the author finds flaws in Snowdon's argument, pointing out that surveys consistently underestimate calorie consumption and that there are various reasons for this, such as shame, desire to lose weight, snacking habits, portion size discrepancies, and under-reporting of food waste.

The chapter concludes with the author discussing the work of Herman Pontzer, who studied the daily energy expenditure of hunter-gatherers, farmers, and sedentary office workers. Surprisingly, the study found that the calories burned by hunter-gatherers were similar to those of American and European populations, challenging the belief that reduced physical activity is the sole driver of weight gain.

Workbook:

Discussion Questions:

1. How does the perception that obesity is caused by a lack of exercise influence societal attitudes towards individuals living with obesity?

----

2. What are the potential implications of focusing solely on physical activity as a solution to weight gain?

----

3. How do societal factors, such as the availability of ultra-processed foods and sedentary lifestyles, contribute to the obesity epidemic?

----

4. How can we encourage a more balanced approach to addressing weight gain, considering both diet and exercise?

Lessons:

> Weight gain is a complex issue influenced by various factors, including diet, physical activity, and societal conditions.
> Relying solely on exercise to counteract the effects of a poor diet may not be effective in preventing weight gain.

> ➤ Underestimating calorie consumption in surveys can skew data and lead to misconceptions about the relationship between diet and weight.

Action Steps:

> ➤ Reflect on your own eating and exercise habits. Are there any changes you could make to achieve a healthier balance?
> ➤ Educate yourself about the nutritional content of foods and strive to make informed choices.
> ➤ Advocate for policies that promote access to nutritious foods and encourage physical activity in communities.

Journal Prompts:

> ➤ How does your personal experience align with or challenge the idea that exercise is the primary driver of weight gain or loss?
> ➤ Reflect on any societal or cultural influences that may have shaped your beliefs about weight, exercise, and diet.
> ➤ Write about a time when you felt judged or stigmatized based on your weight or physical appearance.

9.

........or about willpower.

In this chapter, the author discusses the misconception around willpower and its relation to weight gain. There is a prevalent belief that individuals can override their internal food intake regulation system through sheer willpower. This idea is particularly associated with weight gain and obesity, while other diet-related diseases like cancer or cardiovascular disease are not attributed to lack of willpower. The author explores the genetic factors contributing to obesity and explains that while rare genetic defects can cause unavoidable weight gain, the majority of people with obesity have minor genetic differences that affect eating behavior.

The author shares personal experiences with his twin brother, who has been significantly heavier despite sharing the same genetic code and having similar genetic risk factors for obesity. The difference in weight between them is attributed to environmental factors rather than willpower. The author highlights the influence of the food environment, particularly the presence of ultra-processed foods (UPF) and the marketing strategies employed by fast-food companies. Food swamps, characterized by a high density of fast-food outlets and limited access to fresh and healthy food options, contribute to unhealthy eating habits.

The author emphasizes the impact of advertising on food choices, especially among children. Adver-games, which promote UPF consumption, have been shown to increase the intake of nutrient-poor snacks and reduce the consumption of fruits and vegetables. The author discusses the significant influence of the fast-food industry on youth culture and the need for healthier food environments. Poverty and chronic stress are identified as additional factors that contribute to weight gain, as stress increases the secretion of cortisol, a hormone associated with increased appetite for UPF.

The chapter concludes by highlighting the complex interaction between genes, environment, and willpower. The heritability of obesity is influenced by the food environment, with higher-income households providing some protection against obesity. The author suggests that addressing poverty could significantly reduce the risk of obesity. The chapter underscores the importance of considering factors beyond willpower and exploring regulatory measures and pricing strategies to promote healthier food choices.

Workbook:
Discussion Questions:

1.How does the concept of willpower contribute to the stigma associated with weight gain and obesity?

----

2. What role does the food environment play in shaping eating behaviors and food choices?

----

3. How can advertising impact children's food preferences and consumption habits?

----

4. In what ways can poverty and chronic stress contribute to weight gain and obesity?

Lessons:

➢ Willpower alone is not sufficient to overcome the complex factors contributing to weight gain and obesity.
➢ Genetic factors influence eating behavior, but the environment plays a significant role in determining weight outcomes.
➢ The presence of ultra-processed foods and the marketing strategies of fast-food companies contribute to unhealthy eating habits.
➢ Addressing poverty and creating healthier food environments are crucial in reducing the risk of obesity.

Action Steps:

➢ Educate yourself about the influence of the food environment and marketing tactics on your food choices.
➢ Advocate for policies and regulations that promote healthier food options in your community.

➤ Support initiatives aimed at reducing poverty and improving access to nutritious foods for disadvantaged populations.

➤ Practice mindful eating and develop strategies to make healthier choices despite environmental challenges.

Journal Prompts:

➤ Reflect on a time when you felt judged or stigmatized based on your weight or eating habits. How did this experience impact you?

➤ Describe your typical food environment and its influence on your eating habits. Are there any changes you would like to make?

➤ Explore your personal beliefs about willpower and weight gain. How do these beliefs align with the information presented in the chapter?

➤ Consider the role of advertising in shaping your food preferences. Are there any specific advertisements or marketing tactics that have influenced your choices?

10.

How UPF hacks our brains.

In this chapter the author shares his experiences and insights regarding ultra-processed foods (UPF). He starts by reminiscing about frozen meals and their rise in popularity, particularly TV dinners, which became ubiquitous in the US. The author notes that the UK now consumes more ready meals than any other European country. He then describes his own diet during the third week, highlighting the challenges of eating UPF while being aware of its potential harms.

The author discusses the addictive nature of UPF, citing research that shows how certain combinations of salt, fat, sugar, and protein can activate the brain's reward system, similar to how drugs like alcohol or nicotine affect the brain. He explores the concept of "wanting" and how positive experiences with food can lead to constant cravings. Additionally, he delves into the composition of UPF, explaining how these foods are often reconstructed from basic molecular constituents, heavily modified, and assembled into food-like shapes and textures.

The author acknowledges the limitations of the NOVA classification system for evaluating individual foods, emphasizing that while some products may technically not be classified as UPF, they still possess properties and additives that may be harmful. He discusses the importance of considering the overall dietary pattern rather than focusing solely on individual foods. The author also describes his search for "healthier" UPF options, including switching to diet drinks and choosing lasagnas with fewer additives.

After completing his UPF diet, the author undergoes testing, revealing significant weight gain, disrupted appetite hormones, increased inflammation markers, and notable changes in brain connectivity. He reflects on the conflicting thoughts and desires he experienced during the diet, with his brain's reward system craving UPF despite his growing knowledge of its harms. The author expresses concern about the impact of UPF on children and teenagers, as their developing brains are more vulnerable to the effects of these foods.

Workbook:

Discussion Questions:

1. Have you ever noticed any addictive tendencies towards ultra-processed foods? What are some of the factors that contribute to this?

----

2. How do you think the widespread availability and marketing of UPF impact our food choices and eating behaviors?

----

3. What strategies can individuals employ to reduce their consumption of ultra-processed foods and make healthier choices?

----

4. How can society as a whole work towards reducing the prevalence and impact of UPF on public health?

Lessons:

> ➤ Ultra-processed foods can have an addictive nature due to their specific combinations of salt, fat, sugar, and protein.
> ➤ UPF often lack recognizable real food components and are heavily processed, containing numerous additives.
> ➤ The NOVA classification system provides a broad understanding of dietary patterns but has limitations in evaluating individual foods.
> ➤ Consuming UPF can lead to weight gain, hormonal imbalances, and changes in brain connectivity.
> ➤ Awareness of the harmful effects of UPF can influence individuals' food choices and desire to make healthier decisions.
> ➤ The impact of UPF on children and teenagers, especially during their developmental years, is a significant concern that requires further research.

Action Steps:

➢ Assess your current consumption of ultra-processed foods and identify areas where you can make healthier choices.

➢ Explore alternative options to UPF, such as whole, minimally processed foods, and experiment with cooking and preparing meals at home.

➢ Read ingredient labels and become familiar with common additives found in UPF to make more informed food choices.

➢ Educate yourself and others about the addictive nature of UPF and its potential health consequences.

Journal Prompts:

➢ Reflect on a time when you experienced cravings for UPF and how it affected your eating habits.

➢ Describe any changes you have noticed in your own brain's response to food after reducing or eliminating UPF from your diet.

➢ Consider the impact of UPF on children and teenagers and brainstorm ways

PART THREE: Oh, so this is why I'm anxious
and my belly aches!

11.

UPF is pre-chewed

In this chapter, the author explores the concept of the food matrix and its implications for our bodies. Anthony Fardet, a scientist, introduces the idea that food is not simply the sum of its nutrients but is affected by its physical structure or matrix. The purpose of the digestive system is to destroy this matrix. The author discusses an experiment from 1977 that compared the impact of apple juice, apple puree, and whole apples on blood sugar, insulin levels, and satiety. The study found that whole apples led to a slower and steadier rise in blood sugar, sustained satiety, while the juice and puree caused rapid spikes and crashes, leaving the participants still feeling hungry.

The author then explains how ultra-processed foods (UPF) are designed to be soft and easily chewable, resembling pre-chewed food. The softness is achieved by mechanically processing plant components and meats until fibrous textures are destroyed, making it easy to consume quickly. UPF, despite containing fiber and other constituents, can be as calorie-dense as they absorb quickly in the body, which may not trigger the 'stop eating' signals in the gut, leading to overeating.

The chapter also delves into the impact of UPF on dental health. The softness of these foods means less chewing, which might be contributing to modern dental issues like overbites and impacted wisdom teeth.

Furthermore, the calorie density and softness of UPF may lead to increased calorie intake and higher risk of weight gain and metabolic diseases. The speed at which we eat is influenced by genetic factors, and some individuals may be more vulnerable to the effects of UPF due to their genes.

The author raises concern about the possibility of creating UPF with textures designed to slow down consumption without addressing the underlying issues of processed food.

Workbook:

Discussion Questions:

1. How does the concept of the food matrix challenge our understanding of nutrition and the way we should approach our diets?

----

2. In what ways does the softness and pre-chewed nature of ultra-processed foods contribute to overeating and weight gain?

----

3. How can we encourage people to shift away from ultra-processed foods and choose more whole, less processed options?

----

4. What are some possible solutions or innovations that could address the issues raised in this chapter regarding the impact of UPF on our bodies?

Lessons:

> ➢ The physical structure of food, known as the food matrix, plays a significant role in how our bodies respond to and digest different foods.
> ➢ Ultra-processed foods (UPF) are designed to be soft and easily chewable, leading to quick consumption and potential overeating.
> ➢ UPF's calorie density and rapid absorption may hinder the 'stop eating' signals in the gut, leading to continued hunger and increased calorie intake.
> ➢ Dental health can be affected by the lack of chewing in UPF, contributing to dental

problems like overbites and impacted wisdom teeth.

➤ The energy density of food is a crucial factor in moderating daily energy intake and may contribute to weight gain.

➤ The rate at which we consume food can be influenced by genetics, and certain eating styles may make some individuals more susceptible to the effects of UPF.

Action Steps:

➤ Incorporate more whole foods into your diet, such as fresh fruits and vegetables, to benefit from their natural food matrix.

➤ Choose less-processed bread options, like sourdough or real bread, which require more chewing and provide better dental health benefits.

➤ Be mindful of your eating speed and try to slow down, allowing your body to recognize fullness signals.

➤ Read food labels and opt for lower-energy-density options to help moderate your calorie intake.

12.

UPF smells funny

In this chapter the author explores the impact of artificial flavoring on overconsumption and obesity. He meets Barry Smith, a philosopher, food scientist, and expert in the study of smell and taste. Barry explains that our senses of taste, smell, and flavor are interconnected, and food companies exploit these connections to make ultra-processed foods (UPFs) more appealing.

Barry demonstrates how color influences the perception of taste and smell in wine experts, leading them to misidentify wines based on added dyes. He reveals some of the sensory tricks UPF manufacturers use, like adding caramel scent to ice cream bar wrappers to trigger cravings. The complexity of flavor lies in the brain's integration of inputs from various senses, memories, and expectations.

Smell plays a crucial role in determining the safety and nutritional value of food. Humans can distinguish between an astonishing number of smells, over a trillion. Smell also influences taste, and UPF manufacturers take advantage of this by using secret flavor profiles paired with high levels of fats and sugars to build brand loyalty from a young age.

Workbook:
Discussion Questions:

> ➤ In what ways can food companies manipulate our senses to make UPFs more appealing? How can consumers become more aware of these tactics?

> ➤ Discuss the possible long-term effects of consuming UPFs with artificial flavorings on public health.

> ➤ How might a deeper understanding of the science of taste and smell influence the way we approach food and nutrition education in schools and households?

Lessons:

> ➤ Flavor is a complex interplay of taste, smell, touch, and visual cues, leading to our perception of food.
> ➤ UPF manufacturers use artificial flavorings to create addictive foods, leading to overconsumption and potential health issues.
> ➤ Our sense of smell plays a vital role in determining the safety and nutritional value of food.

➤ Awareness of sensory manipulation can empower consumers to make healthier food choices.

Action Steps:

➤ Pay attention to the ingredients in the foods you consume and avoid those with excessive artificial flavorings.
➤ Experiment with cooking and using natural herbs and spices to enhance the flavors of your dishes.
➤ Educate friends and family about the effects of artificial flavorings on health and encourage them to make informed food choices.

Journal Prompts:

➤ Describe a memorable food experience that involved both taste and smell. How did these senses complement each other?
➤ Think of a favorite childhood treat that you still enjoy today. Reflect on how its flavor and scent influence your perception of it.
➤ Consider the impact of color on your food choices. Are there certain colors that make you more likely to try a particular food?

13.

UPF tastes odd

In this chapter the author explores the science behind taste and flavor enhancers in ultra-processed foods (UPFs). He discusses his conversation with a chemistry professor, Andrea Sella, about the presence of flavor enhancers like glutamate, guanylate, and inosinate in Pringles. These molecules stimulate receptors in the mouth and signal the presence of easily digestible protein. However, UPFs like Pringles lack the nutritional value associated with these molecules.

The chapter delves into the anatomy of taste, explaining that taste buds are small pits found on papillae in the mouth. There are specialized cells within taste buds that detect molecules in food, convert them into signals, and send them to the brain. The author highlights that taste receptors are not only present in the mouth but also in other parts of the body.

The five basic tastes – sweet, umami, sour, salt, and bitter – are discussed, along with their corresponding receptors and the foods that activate them. The author explains how taste interactions can affect our enjoyment of food.

For example, combining sweet and sour flavors can be appealing, as it signals the presence of ripe, vitamin-C-rich fruit.

The chapter also explores how UPF manufacturers use flavor enhancement to make their products more palatable. They combine sweet, sour, salt, and umami flavors to enhance the overall taste, tricking our senses and making us crave more. The author uses the example of Coca-Cola, which combines bitterness from caffeine with extreme sweetness, sourness, fizziness, and coldness to mask the bitterness and allow for a high sugar content.

Additionally, the author mentions the addictive nature of sugar and how the body's aversion to excessive sugar consumption might be a protective mechanism. UPFs exploit taste interactions to create sensory confusion and make us consume more sugar. The author references studies that show how our preference for flavors is influenced by changes in blood glucose levels.

The chapter concludes by highlighting the pricing phenomenon of sweet fizzy beverages being cheaper than bottled water in low-income countries. The author suggests that UPFs, by speed balling different tastes and sensations, can deliver excessive calories and create neurological rewards that keep us coming back for more.

Workbook:
Discussion Questions:

1. How do UPFs manipulate taste to make them more appealing to consumers?

----

2. What are some examples of natural foods rich in the flavor enhancers glutamate, guanylate, and inosinate?

----

3. Why do you think UPFs can be addictive, leading people to consume them in large quantities?

----

4. How can we train ourselves to enjoy more natural and unprocessed foods, even when they might not have the same intense flavors as UPFs?

Lessons:

> ➤ Understand the impact of flavor enhancers: Learn about the effects of glutamate, guanylate, and inosinate on taste and how they can influence our desire for certain foods.
> ➤ Recognize the importance of real nutrition: Acknowledge the significance of consuming whole, nutrient-rich foods instead of relying on UPFs with empty calories and artificial flavors.
> ➤ Be mindful of taste interactions: Be aware of how different tastes can influence each other and affect your overall enjoyment of food.
> ➤ Limit UPF consumption: Reduce your intake of ultra-processed foods to promote a healthier diet and lifestyle.

Action Steps:

> ➤ Conduct a taste experiment: Try a variety of natural foods with glutamate, guanylate, and inosinate, and compare their flavors with UPFs that contain these flavor enhancers. Take note of the differences in taste and satisfaction.
> ➤ Cook homemade meals: Prepare meals using fresh, unprocessed ingredients to

enjoy the natural flavors and nutritional benefits of real food.

➢ Seek alternatives for cravings: When craving UPFs, find healthier alternatives that still satisfy your taste preferences but are less processed and more nutritious.

Journal Prompts:

➢ Describe a time when you noticed the taste of a UPF was different from natural food. How did it make you feel, both physically and emotionally?

➢ Write about a favorite homemade dish that you enjoy. How do the natural flavors of its ingredients contribute to your enjoyment?

➢ Reflect on your daily eating habits. Are there specific UPFs that you consume regularly? How might you reduce their intake?

14.

Additive anxiety

In this chapter, the author explores the concept of taste and flavor enhancers in ultra-processed foods (UPF). They engage in a discussion with Andrea Sella, an Italian professor of chemistry, to understand why flavor enhancers like glutamate, guanylate, and inosinate are present in UPF such as Pringles. Andrea explains that these molecules are associated with easily digestible protein and are the signature of fermented fish, plants, meaty broths, and vintage cheese. These molecules stimulate the receptors in the mouth, signaling the presence of nutrition. In contrast, UPF like Pringles lack these molecules and rely on other taste elements to create a sensory experience.

The chapter further delves into the science behind taste, highlighting the presence of taste buds and papillae on the tongue. Taste buds contain specialized cells with receptors that detect molecules in food and send signals to the brain. The author explains the five main tastes: sweet, umami (savoury), sour, salt, and bitter. There may also be specific tastes for water, starch, maltodextrins, calcium, metals, and fatty acids, although further research is needed. The author discusses how different tastes interact with each other and how manufacturers of UPF use flavor enhancement techniques to make their products more appealing.

The example of Coca-Cola is used to illustrate this phenomenon. The original formula contained bitter components like coca leaves and caffeine, which were masked by adding large amounts of sugar. The combination of bitterness, sourness from phosphoric acid, cold temperature, and fizziness allows a significant amount of sugar to be consumed without triggering aversion. The author likens this sensory confusion to "speedballing," a term used in drug use to describe the simultaneous consumption of sedatives and stimulants.

The chapter also explores how the association between flavors and calories affects human preferences. Studies have shown that humans develop preferences for flavors based on how much their blood glucose levels change when consuming them. The author suggests that UPF manufacturers use the combination of taste elements in their products, along with a spike in blood glucose, to make consumers crave their specific products. This may explain the pricing phenomenon observed in low-income countries, where sweet fizzy beverages are often cheaper than bottled water.

In addition to the issue of excessive sugar consumption, the author highlights the concern regarding zero-calorie artificial sweeteners. They raise the question of what happens when the taste in our mouths does not match the calorie content of the food or drink.

Workbook:

Discussion Questions:

1. How do flavor enhancers in ultra-processed foods affect our perception of taste and nutrition?

----

2. What are the potential consequences of sensory confusion caused by UPF on our overall health?

----

3. Do you think the combination of taste elements used in UPF is a deliberate strategy by manufacturers to make us consume more? Why or why not?

----

4. How can we develop healthier eating habits and reduce our reliance on ultra-processed foods?

Lessons and Action Steps:

➢ Lesson: Understanding the science of taste can help us make informed food choices.
  o Action Step: Research more about taste receptors and the role they play in food preferences.
➢ Lesson: Ultra-processed foods often use flavor enhancement to create addictive products.

- o Action Step: Start reading food labels to identify hidden additives and flavor enhancers in processed foods.
- ➢ Lesson: Combining various tastes can make food more enjoyable.
  - o Action Step: Experiment with healthy recipes that combine different tastes like sweet, sour, and savory.
- ➢ Lesson: High sugar content in ultra-processed foods can create a craving cycle.
  - o Action Step: Reduce your intake of sugary drinks and snacks and opt for natural sweeteners when needed.
- ➢ Lesson: Ultra-processed foods lack real nutrition.
  - o Action Step: Focus on a balanced diet with whole, nutrient-rich foods to ensure better health.
- ➢ Lesson: Being mindful of taste and flavor can lead to better eating habits.
  - o Action Step: Practice mindful eating by savoring each bite and paying attention to taste sensations.

PART FOUR: But I already paid for this!

15.

Dysregulatory bodies

In this chapter the author explores the regulation of food additives in the United States. The author initially assumes that food additives go through a rigorous testing and approval process similar to that of pharmaceutical drugs. However, upon researching the topic, they discover significant gaps in the regulatory system.

The author consults experts Maricel Maffini and Tom Neltner, who explain the process of regulating food additives using the example of COZ corn oil. This oil was extracted from corn mash used in ethanol biofuel production and contained antibiotics and other additives. The company producing the oil wanted to market it for human consumption, which meant it had to be considered a new food additive.

There are three options for bringing a new additive to the market. The first option involves a full review by the FDA, which requires submitting extensive data and can take several years. The second option is to apply for a "generally recognized as safe" (GRAS) notification, where the company voluntarily submits data to the FDA, and if there are no follow-up questions, the additive is considered safe. The third option is self-determination, where companies can withdraw their FDA application and market the additive based on their own determination of safety.

The author discovers that the self-determination route is commonly used, with the majority of new food chemicals being self-determined by companies. This process allows companies to bypass FDA scrutiny and make their own safety decisions, even though there are significant deficiencies in testing and evaluation. The lack of comprehensive regulation and oversight raises concerns about the safety of food additives.

The chapter also highlights the issue of flavors, which are regulated by the Flavor and Extract Manufacturers Association (FEMA). FEMA has its own GRAS determination process independent of the FDA. This self-regulation raises concerns, as exemplified by the case of isoeugenol, a flavoring substance certified GRAS by FEMA despite clear evidence of causing liver cancer in mice.

Workbook:

Discussion Questions:

1. How does the self-determination process for food additives affect consumer safety? What are the potential risks and consequences?

----

2. Should companies be allowed to self-determine the safety of food additives, or should there be stricter regulations and oversight? Discuss the pros and cons of each approach.

----

3. How can consumers make informed choices about the safety of food additives when there are gaps in regulation and limited transparency? What actions can individuals take to protect themselves?

----

4. What role should government agencies play in ensuring the safety of food additives? How can regulatory bodies be improved to address the shortcomings discussed in the chapter?

Lessons and Action Steps:

➢ Understand food labels: Educate yourself about different food additives and their potential health effects. Read labels carefully and opt for products with fewer additives or those that are certified organic and non-GMO.

➢ Engage with policymakers: Write to your local representatives and the FDA expressing your concerns about food additive regulation. Advocate for stricter safety measures and transparency in the approval process.

➢ Support food safety organizations: Contribute to and volunteer with organizations dedicated to promoting food safety and transparency in the food industry.

➢ Promote clean eating: Encourage your family and friends to adopt a diet focused on whole, unprocessed foods. Share recipes and tips for preparing nutritious meals at home.

➢ Educate others: Share the knowledge you've gained about food additives and their potential risks. Start discussions within your community and on social media to spread awareness.

➢ Choose safer alternatives: When possible, opt for natural flavorings and avoid processed foods with excessive additives.

Journal Prompts:

➢ How does learning about the dysregulation of food additives make you feel, and why?

➢ Reflect on your own eating habits. Are there any processed foods you consume regularly? How might this knowledge impact your future food choices?

➢ Imagine a world with stricter food additive regulations. How do you think it would affect public health and the food industry?

➢ What steps can you personally take to contribute to the improvement of food additive regulation in your country?

16.
UPF destroys traditional diets

The chapter discusses the destructive impact of ultra-processed foods (UPF) on traditional diets, using the example of Nestlé's marketing strategies in Brazil. Nestlé, the largest food processing company globally, has targeted emerging markets like Brazil due to saturated markets in Europe and North America. In Brazil, Nestlé has employed novel marketing techniques, including door-to-door sales in slum areas where traditional distribution infrastructure is lacking. The company claims to provide value to society by selling fortified products to lower-income consumers. However, the reality is that customers are mainly interested in sugary items rather than healthy options.

The author shares his experience in Belém, Brazil, where he investigates Nestlé's activities. He discovers the existence of a floating supermarket, Nestlé Até Você a Bordo, which serves remote Amazon communities. The author also witnesses the impact of soy farming on the Amazon rainforest and its connection to the production of UPF. Brazilian soy is extensively used in processed foods worldwide, including the UK.

The author visits Muaná, a town affected by Nestlé's marketing practices. The introduction of low-priced UPF from Nestlé's boat store negatively affects local traders selling whole foods. The availability and demand for UPF have increased, leading to a rise in childhood obesity and diet-related diabetes. The author visits a small supermarket in Muaná that now stocks Nestlé products due to customer demand. Church NGOs and other organizations are attempting to address the public health crisis resulting from UPF consumption.

The chapter concludes by highlighting the violence committed by large food companies like Nestlé, both on human bodies and the environment. The destructive impact of UPF on traditional diets and local economies is evident in Brazil, while similar issues are also present globally.

Workbook:

Discussion Questions:

1. How can food companies strike a balance between business expansion and respecting traditional food cultures?

----

2. What are the consequences of UPF marketing and consumption on vulnerable communities and their health?

----

3. How can governments and NGOs address the challenges posed by the growing influence of UPF in emerging markets?

----

4. Reflect on Nestlé's floating supermarket initiative. Do you think it truly aimed to improve nutrition and wellness, or was it primarily a marketing strategy to expand UPF sales?

Lessons:

➤ The rise of UPF can disrupt traditional diets and harm vulnerable communities by promoting unhealthy eating habits.

➤ Food companies should consider the social and health consequences of their marketing strategies and product offerings.

➤ UPF production, like soy farming, can lead to environmental degradation and contribute to global health issues.

➤ Public awareness and education are crucial in combating the negative effects of UPF on society.

Action Steps:

➤ Investigate the origin of some of your favorite food products. Look for information on their ingredients and nutritional value.

➤ Support local farmers and producers by purchasing whole and minimally processed foods.

➤ Engage in conversations with friends and family about the impact of UPF on health and traditional diets.

➤ Advocate for transparent food labeling and regulations to help consumers make informed choices.

➤ 5.   Reduce your consumption of UPF and incorporate more whole and nutritious foods into your diet.

➤ 6.   Join local initiatives or NGOs that promote sustainable and healthy eating practices.

Journal Prompts:

➤ Describe your experience with UPF and how they may have affected your health or eating habits.

➤ Reflect on a time when you tried a new type of cuisine or food from a different culture. How did it impact your perspective on food?

➤ Consider the environmental implications of UPF production and their impact on the planet. How does this influence your food choices?

➤ Write about a traditional dish or meal that holds cultural significance to you or your community. What does it represent, and why is it essential to preserve such culinary heritage?

17.

UPF Destroys Traditional Diets

In this chapter the author explores the legal battle between Procter & Gamble (P&G), the manufacturers of Pringles, and the British tax authorities over whether Pringles should be classified as potato crisps and subject to value-added tax (VAT). The complex tax laws in the UK regarding food products and VAT exemptions led to this dispute. P&G argued that Pringles should not be considered potato crisps due to their low potato content and unique manufacturing process. They claimed that Pringles were more like cakes and therefore should be exempt from VAT.

The legal case began in 2004 when P&G introduced a new product called Pringles Dippers, which had a scoop shape for dipping into sauces. P&G argued that the act of dipping constituted "further preparation" and thus exempted Pringles Dippers from being categorized as potato crisps. The initial tax tribunal agreed with P&G's argument, setting the stage for further legal battles from 2007 to 2009. Eventually, the court ruled that Pringles were indeed made of potato and should be subject to VAT.

The author highlights how food companies often engage in legal battles to minimize their tax obligations and increase profits. Many other food products have also been involved in similar disputes with the tax authorities. These cases not only cost a significant amount of money but also raise questions about the fairness of the tax system and how taxpayers end up subsidizing certain snacks. The author sees tax avoidance as part of the ultra-processing of food, which aims to create highly profitable products.

Moreover, the chapter discusses the broader costs of ultra-processed foods (UPF), including environmental destruction, antibiotic resistance, and plastic pollution. The production and consumption of UPF contribute to climate change, with emissions from the global food system alone projected to exceed the 1.5°C rise in temperature by 2100. UPF consumption is also linked to environmental damage, such as deforestation for commodity crop production and the use of fertilizers, pesticides, and fossil fuels. The prevalence of UPF in the food system reflects an unhealthy focus on producing as much food as possible, resulting in a decline in food diversity.

Workbook:

Discussion Questions:

1. How does the Pringles court case highlight the challenges in classifying food products for tax purposes? What are the consequences of misclassification?

----

2. Why do you think food companies invest significant resources in legal battles over tax categorization? What motivations might they have for minimizing their tax obligations?

----

3. Discuss the environmental costs associated with UPF. How does the production and consumption of ultra-processed foods contribute to climate change, land use, antibiotic resistance, and plastic pollution?

----

4. What are the ethical considerations surrounding tax avoidance by food companies?

How does it impact public funds and consumer prices?

Lessons:

> ➢ The UK tax system is complex, and the classification of food products for tax purposes can lead to legal disputes.
> ➢ Food companies often employ legal strategies to minimize their tax obligations and maximize profits.
> ➢ Ultra-processed foods have significant environmental costs, including contributions to climate change, land degradation, antibiotic resistance, and plastic pollution.
> ➢ Tax avoidance by food companies can have implications for public funds and consumer prices.

Guides and Action Steps:

➢ Familiarize yourself with the tax regulations surrounding food products in your country. Understand the criteria used to determine tax categories and exemptions.

➢ Support initiatives and organizations that promote sustainable food systems and advocate for transparent and fair taxation practices in the food industry.

➢ Reduce your consumption of ultra-processed foods and opt for whole, unprocessed alternatives whenever possible. Make informed choices about the food products you purchase and their environmental impact.

➢ Stay informed about ongoing legal battles and tax-related issues in the food industry. Support efforts to hold food companies accountable for their environmental and social responsibilities.

Journal Prompts:

➢ Reflect on a time when you became aware of the complexities of the tax system in your country. How did it impact your understanding of the food industry and consumer choices?

18.

UPF is designed to be overconsumed

The chapter explores the science behind how ultra-processed food (UPF) affects the human body and discusses the challenges of reformulating UPF to make it healthier. The author highlights various ways in which UPF impacts our health, including its soft texture that leads to overeating, high calorie density, displacement of whole foods from the diet, addictive properties, damage to the microbiome, and negative effects on satiety and endocrine function. The convenience, price, and marketing of UPF also contribute to excessive consumption.

However, the author argues that the industry's response to these concerns is hyperprocessing or reformulation. The companies add more processing, emulsifiers, and other additives to address the negative effects of UPF. The author questions the effectiveness of reformulation because many UPF products causing diet-related diseases have already been reformulated in the past. Furthermore, UPF is designed to be purchased and consumed in large quantities, making it difficult to reduce consumption through reformulation.

The chapter then delves into the financial incentives driving the production and consumption of UPF. The author interviews individuals within the industry, including a farmer, a former employee of Kellogg's, and an investment banker. The discussion reveals that the food industry operates within a complex ecosystem with multiple layers, including farmers, primary processors, ingredient companies, and multinational corporations. Each layer extracts value and profits from the processing and sale of UPF.

The author emphasizes that companies within the food industry are driven by financial goals and shareholder demands. While some companies strive to meet consumer demands for healthier and sustainable products, financial markets prioritize growth, margins, cash flow, and dividends. CEOs are evaluated based on financial results rather than environmental or sustainability goals. This focus on financial performance leaves food companies with two choices: increase prices and sell fewer units or sell more units to more people more often.

The chapter concludes by highlighting the challenges in changing the food industry's practices and the need for a deeper understanding of the incentives and motivations driving the production and consumption of UPF. Real change may require addressing the systemic issues within the industry rather than relying solely on reformulation efforts.

Workbook:

Discussion Questions:

1. What are the main factors that contribute to the addictive nature of Ultra-Processed Food?

----

2. How can individuals make healthier food choices in an environment dominated by convenience and marketing of UPF?

----

3. What role do government policies play in regulating the food industry and promoting healthier food options?

----

4. How can the food industry be incentivized to prioritize the production of healthier, minimally processed foods?

Lessons:

➤ Understanding the science behind UPF consumption helps individuals make informed choices about their diets.
➤ Reformulation of UPF is not a long-term solution to combat its adverse effects on health.
➤ The food industry's profit-driven approach often prioritizes hyperprocessing and marketing over public health concerns.
➤ Developing a deeper understanding of the food value chain highlights the

complexity of the UPF problem and the various stakeholders involved.

➢ Educating consumers about the hidden effects of UPF consumption empowers them to make healthier choices for themselves and their families.

➢ Government intervention and regulations can play a significant role in promoting healthier food environments.

Guides & Action Steps:

➢ Create a list of common UPF products in your diet and find healthier alternatives with similar flavors and textures.

➢ Develop a meal plan based on whole, minimally processed foods, and try cooking at least one new recipe each week.

➢ Research and support food companies that prioritize sustainability and ethical sourcing.

➢ Advocate for clearer food labeling and more transparent information about UPF ingredients.

➢ Encourage local initiatives and policies that promote access to fresh, nutritious foods in low-income communities.

Journal Prompts:

➤ Describe a time when you felt compelled to consume UPF. What emotions or circumstances influenced your choice?
➤ Reflect on a time when you made a conscious effort to avoid UPF. How did it make you feel, physically and emotionally?
➤ Consider the role of marketing and advertising in shaping your food preferences and choices. How might you resist their influence?
➤ Write about any challenges you face in avoiding UPF and brainstorm strategies to overcome them.

Conclusion: In conclusion, "Ultra-Processed People: Why We Can't Stop Eating Food That Isn't Food" presents a detailed analysis of the impact of UPF on human health and the food industry. The chapter sheds light on the complexities of the food value chain, exposing the financial incentives that drive the production and consumption of UPF. Armed with this knowledge, individuals can take action to make healthier food choices, advocate for transparency in the food industry, and support sustainable and ethical practices. Additionally, urging

19.

What we could ask governments to do

In this chapter, the author discusses the aggressive marketing practices of the infant formula industry and the impact they have had on global health. The author recounts the story of Carlos Monteiro, who witnessed the marketing tactics of formula companies while studying infant malnutrition. Sales representatives, dressed as "mothercraft nurses," promoted formula in low-income settings where access to clean water and literacy rates were low, leading to thousands of avoidable deaths. The author highlights the unethical practices of formula companies, including marketing breastfeeding as insufficient and promoting formula in communities where it was difficult to produce safe and uncontaminated feeds. The author emphasizes the importance of limiting the marketing of formula as the most effective intervention for preventing child deaths.

The chapter also discusses the influence of the formula industry on policy-making and the need to remove their conflict of interest. The author argues that policymakers should not take money from the food industry and should instead have an adversarial relationship with them to protect public health. The author criticizes the involvement of food companies in shaping nutrition policy and highlights the importance of unbiased regulation.

Workbook:
Discussion Questions:

1. What are the consequences of aggressive marketing practices by the infant formula industry in low-income settings?

----

2. Why is it important to limit the marketing of formula and ensure access to accurate information about feeding options?

----

3. How can policymakers and healthcare professionals avoid conflicts of interest when making decisions about infant feeding policies?

----

4. What are some potential strategies for reducing the influence of the food industry on policy-making and promoting public health?

Lessons:

> ➢ Aggressive marketing practices by the infant formula industry have led to avoidable deaths and increased rates of pneumonia and diarrhea in low-income settings.
> ➢ Limiting the marketing of formula is the most effective intervention for preventing child deaths and promoting breastfeeding.
> ➢ Policymakers and healthcare professionals should avoid conflicts of

interest and have an adversarial relationship with the food industry to protect public health.

➤ Access to accurate information about feeding options is essential for parents to make informed choices about their children's nutrition.

➤ The formula industry's influence on policy-making hinders the implementation of effective strategies to address diet-related diseases.

➤ Removing the influence of the food industry from policy-making is crucial for promoting public health and reducing the burden of diet-related illnesses.

Action Steps:

➤ Advocate for policies that limit the marketing of infant formula and ensure access to accurate information about feeding options.

➤ Support organizations and initiatives that promote breastfeeding and provide resources for parents who choose to use formula.

➤ Educate healthcare professionals and policymakers about the ethical concerns regarding conflicts of interest with the food industry.

➢ Encourage transparency in policy-making processes and ensure that decisions are based on unbiased scientific evidence.
➢ Engage in public discourse and raise awareness about the impact of aggressive marketing practices on global health.

Journal Prompts:

➢ Reflect on your own feeding choices or experiences as a parent. How have marketing practices influenced your decisions?
➢ Consider the ethical implications of the aggressive marketing of infant formula in low-income settings. How can these practices be addressed on a global scale?
➢ How do conflicts of interest between the food industry and policymakers affect public health outcomes? What steps can be taken to mitigate these conflicts?
➢ Share your thoughts on the importance of access to accurate information about feeding options for parents. How can this information be effectively communicated and made available to all?

20.

What to do if you want to stop eating UPF

In this chapter, the author provides guidance for individuals who want to stop eating ultra-processed foods (UPF). The author suggests starting with an 80 percent UPF diet for a few days to understand and grapple with the concept of UPF. They encourage readers to become familiar with the NOVA 4 definition of UPF and to recognize the presence of additives and industrially produced substances in the food they consume.

For those who suspect they have an addictive relationship with UPF, the author recommends taking the Yale Food Addiction Scale test to assess their level of addiction. If addiction is identified, seeking help from friends, relatives, or doctors is advised. Alternatively, individuals may choose to eat some UPF while avoiding problem products and identifying vulnerable moments and foods that may trigger a binge.

The author and Xand, the author's companion, have found abstinence to be the most effective approach to overcoming their addiction to UPF. Xand managed to lose around 20kg in a few months by completely quitting UPF and remains abstinent with no exceptions. The author acknowledges that UPF is merely a substance through which other underlying problems are realized, and addressing these issues may be necessary before effectively tackling UPF addiction. Seeking help is encouraged for dealing with these underlying problems.

When transitioning away from UPF, the author acknowledges that it may require more time and money to prepare meals using whole foods. They recommend cookbooks by Allegra McEvedy and Jack Monroe, as their recipes are cheap, easy, and delicious. Cooking meals is described as a hassle but a connection to a long chain of time-hassled humans who have survived long enough to pass on their knowledge.

Weight loss is not the primary focus of the book, but the author shares the experience of Barry Smith, who quit UPF and discovered that moderation was necessary even when consuming natural foods. The author highlights that our addiction to ultra-processed products extends beyond food to various other engineered products that drive excess consumption. They suggest considering abstinence from these products as well, if beneficial.

Finally, the author encourages readers to take ownership of their decisions and experiences, not to be too hard on themselves, and to stay in touch and share their progress.

Workbook:

Discussion Questions:

1. Have you ever attempted to reduce or eliminate ultra-processed foods from your diet? What were your experiences and challenges?

----

2. Do you believe you have an addictive relationship with certain processed foods?

How does this impact your ability to make healthier choices?

----

3. How do you think abstaining from ultra-processed foods could positively affect your physical and mental health?

----

4. In what ways do you think the engineered products and media influence our consumption habits and addiction to certain substances?

Lessons:

➢ Experiment with an 80 percent ultra-processed food diet to better understand its impact on your body and identify addictive relationships with specific foods.
➢ Seek help if you suspect you have a food addiction by taking the Yale Food Addiction Scale test and reaching out to supportive individuals or professionals.
➢ Consider a personalized approach to reducing ultra-processed food consumption, such as avoiding problem

products or practicing abstinence altogether.
➤ Recognize that ultra-processed foods may be a reflection of deeper issues and address these underlying problems with the help of others if necessary.

Action Steps:

➤ Research and take the Yale Food Addiction Scale test to assess the presence of a food addiction.
➤ Reach out to a friend, relative, or healthcare professional for support and guidance in reducing or eliminating ultra-processed foods.
➤ Identify vulnerable moments and foods that may lead to excessive consumption and create strategies to avoid or moderate their intake.
➤ Explore cookbooks by Allegra McEvedy and Jack Monroe to find affordable and delicious recipes for healthier meals.
➤ Assess the influence of engineered products and media on your consumption habits and consider reducing or abstaining from certain items that promote excess consumption.
➤ Track your progress and make note of any positive changes in your physical and

mental well-being as you reduce your intake of ultra-processed foods.

Journal Prompts:

➢ How do you feel about your current eating habits and the role of ultra-processed foods in your diet?

➢ Describe any instances where you felt out of control or addicted to certain processed foods. How did these experiences affect your overall well-being?

➢ Reflect on a time when you successfully reduced or eliminated ultra-processed foods from your diet. What strategies did you use, and how did it make you feel?

➢ Consider the potential benefits of reducing your consumption of ultra-processed foods. How do you envision this positively impacting your life, health, and relationships?

Made in the USA
Monee, IL
19 September 2024

66178377R00069